FAMILY ISSUES AND YOU™

DEALING WITH YOUR PARENTS' DIVORCE

JERRY MCLAUGHLIN
AND KATHERINE E. KROHN

rosen publishing's
rosen central®

NEW YORK

Published in 2016 by The Rosen Publishing Group, Inc.
29 East 21st Street, New York, NY 10010

Copyright © 2016 by The Rosen Publishing Group, Inc.

First Edition

Library of Congress Cataloging-in-Publication Data

McLaughlin, Jerry, 1980-
 Dealing with your parents' divorce / Jerry McLaughlin and Katherine E. Krohn. – First edition.
     pages cm. – (Family issues and you)
 Includes index.
 ISBN 978-1-4994-3711-9 (library bound) – ISBN 978-1-4994-3709-6 (pbk.) – ISBN 978-1-4994-3710-2 (6-pack)
 1. Children of divorced parents–Juvenile literature. 2. Divorce–Psychological aspects–Juvenile literature. I. Krohn, Katherine E. II. Title.
 HQ777.5.M3865 2016
 306.89–dc23
                                                                                    2015019908

Manufactured in the United States of America

CONTENTS

INTRODUCTION

The majority of families in the United States today are divorced, according to Divorcesource.com. These families take a myriad of forms, as described by Divorcesource.com, "including divorced with children who reside with one parent and visit the other; remarried, re-coupled, living together, with his and/or her children; single mothers; re-coupled, dating and alone; divorced fathers who visit their children, and lesbian and gay couples with children from a prior relationship."

Although parents feel shattered or liberated by the divorce, their children probably feel terrified and disoriented by the prospect of a change in their stability and happiness.

"It was a Friday evening, and my brother and I were watching a movie. Our mom and dad came into the room and asked us to turn off the TV. Then our dad said, 'Your mom and I are getting a divorce,'" said Ashley, fourteen, a New York middle school student.

"Our mom started to sob, and then my brother started to cry, too. My heart raced and I felt like I couldn't breathe. I couldn't believe that this was happening.

"Our dad then pronounced, 'We still love you . . . we want what is best for you. Your mom and

Divorce can confuse all members of a family. It also causes fear and emotional upheaval in children's lives.

I still love each other, but we just can't live together anymore.'

"I got so mad. I told my dad that what he had said didn't make sense—I mean, I thought married people were supposed to stick with each other, no matter what. My dad tried to hug me, but I pulled away from him.

"Then my mom flew off the handle. She yelled to my dad that she didn't want a divorce, and *she didn't want HER children to think that the divorce was her fault. She screamed that it was my dad's fault they were getting divorced. My dad yelled at her to 'grow up,' and they just kept yelling at each other. I felt sick to my stomach."*

Chances are you know someone whose parents are divorced. Or maybe your own parents are divorced or planning to get a divorce. If so, you know firsthand how difficult the changes that come with a divorce can be.

This resource is written for people like you who are going through a hard time because of divorce. It will help you sort out your feelings, understand the divorce process a little better, and point you in the right direction to seek out further help. Divorce can change your living situation, and it can affect the family finances and where you go to school. Some changes may be more challenging to get used to than others. Over time you can grow to accept these changes and learn some helpful strategies to deal with them.

CHAPTER ONE

DEFINING DIVORCE AND UNDERSTANDING YOUR FEELINGS

A divorce is the legal end of a marriage. According to 2011 data reported by the Centers for Disease Control and Prevention, there were 2,118,000 marriages in the United States. The marriage rate was 6.8 per 1,000 of the total US population, and the divorce rate was 3.6 per 1,000 of the US population (with forty-four states and the District of Columbia reporting). A 2011 study compiled by the Williams Institute, a gay legal organization located at the University of California in Los Angeles, said that about 1 percent of the total number of married or registered same-sex couples get divorced every year, compared to 2 percent of the number of married straight couples. *Scientific American* reported that there were 1.5

Research suggests that children are more affected by their parents' relationship than by their sexual orientation.

million young people whose parents divorce every year in the United States.

A divorce occurs when two married people decide that they can't live together happily anymore. It can happen to anyone. The couple sign legal papers that end the marriage. Once single, they are free to marry someone else if they want to.

Divorce brings life changes and emotional challenges to everyone in the family. Kids of divorce often have to adjust to new routines. Mealtime and homework routines can change. Sometimes young people have to move when their parents divorce. They may have to attend a new school or live in a new home. Relatives and friends who were once close now may be farther away.

AN EMOTIONAL ROLLER COASTER

If your parents are getting divorced, you may think that you are the only person who feels like you do. In reality, the opposite is true. Studies show that close to 50 percent of marriages in the United States end in divorce. Although everyone's personal story is different, "kids of divorce" know how you feel. You are not alone.

Children of divorcing parents may feel like they are on an emotional roller coaster—with frequent, stomach-churning, ups and downs. They may feel angry, sad, rejected, confused, guilty, or even ashamed.

"Whenever you feel overwhelmed or ashamed about your parents' divorce," says author Rachel Aydt in *Why Me? A Teen Guide to Divorce and Your Feelings*, "remember that you are not a freak who is living through something so horrible,

It is common to feel angry, guilty, and rejected during your parents' divorce. Remember that divorce will not destroy your family; it does change it, though.

bizarre, and upsetting that no one else can relate to your situation. More people than you can imagine have already lived through this."

WHEN DIVORCE IS NOT ALWAYS BAD FOR FAMILY MEMBERS

Although divorce can seem like the worst thing in the world, in reality it can be for the best. Living in a family where the

Children who witness their parents' arguments and fights tend to adapt to life after a divorce better than those who haven't. They find that an atmosphere with less conflict is actually liberating.

parents argue frequently can cause a lot of stress and anxiety. Silent wars—when parents don't fight, instead preferring to ignore each other—can be harmful, too. Even though your parents may not be yelling, they still may not be getting along.

Not all kids feel upset or sad when their parents divorce. Some kids even feel relieved. Montana State University researcher Chelsea Elander asked kids how they really felt about their parents' divorce. "The overwhelming comment was, 'Don't stay together if you are not happy . . . We don't want to live in that environment.'"

"Parents that remain married 'for the sake of the children' may, for all intents and purposes, be emotionally divorced," says social worker Gayle Peterson. Although Peterson believes that married people should try to work through marital problems before they consider divorce, she doesn't believe that divorce is always "bad" for a family.

WHEN PARENTS FIGHT—THE EFFECTS ON TEENS

As arguing and hostility between your parents increase, so may your sense of unhappiness with your family's circumstances. After all, a home should be a place of shelter, unconditional love, and security. However, these characteristics may no longer be feasible to you and your siblings if your parents aren't getting along well. These "missing" qualities that enable a stable home life can have an impact on the whole household. Although you might be suffering quietly for a long time, not knowing how to deal with the fighting going on around you, you might become hardened by your parents' arguing over time. Nevertheless, the long periods of time in which you witness your parents' hostilities toward each other still do not eliminate the desire you might have for closeness and belonging as a complete family unit.

A study conducted by psychologist E. Mavis Hetherington at the University of Virginia found that some kids who are exposed to a lot of marital fighting before a divorce actually adjust better than those who experience low levels of conflict. These children who have witnessed high levels of fighting between parents before a divorce experience the divorce as a huge relief from their parents' arguing.

THE INITIAL PERIOD OF SHOCK AND CONFUSION

Divorce can be a very difficult experience in many ways and it can cause many stumbling blocks during its various stages.

It is natural to feel confused about your parents' divorce. In fact, it is normal to feel whatever emotions you are experiencing. You may have a friend whose parents are getting divorced who is moody and prone to crying a lot. On the other hand, you may feel angry and anxious. There are no wrong reactions to a divorce. Regardless of what kinds of emotions you are experiencing, it is important that you know that you can and will get through this challenging time in your life. Your family relationships will be different in some ways than before the divorce, but different does not always mean that your situation will be worse. The initial period of shock and confusion that you are experiencing will pass and your loving relationships with your family members can and do continue.

CHAPTER TWO

THE BLAME GAME

It's common to look for an explanation for when something bad happens to a family. Young people might look for a reason for their parents' divorce and even for someone to blame. Often children and teens of divorcing parents think they did something to cause their parents' divorce. In addition, even though they might realize that they did not cause their parents' marital problems, they sometimes blame themselves for not being able to stop the divorce from happening. But divorce is never a young person's fault.

The following are several common misconceptions, or untruths, that young people have about divorce:

- My parents are divorcing because I'm a bad kid.
- It was probably my fault that my parents split up.
- If my parents leave each other, they will leave me, too.
- If I act extra good, my parents might get back together.
- If I act up and cause trouble, maybe my parents will get close again.
- My parents stopped loving each other. I guess they will stop loving me, too.

Young people might sometimes act out by behaving badly at school during the stresses of a divorce. They think by doing so, their parents will have to reunite to help them work through behavioral challenges.

Try to remember that your parents' divorce is about your mom and dad's relationship. Your parents split up with each other, not you or your siblings. Some kids hope that acting like the ideal child will bring their parents back together. For the same reason, others behave badly, hoping that their parents will come together to deal with the problems they are creating. However, bad behavior will only make things worse for you and your parents. Acting like a perfect child won't help either.

MOVING FORWARD

Trying to blame one parent, both parents, or yourself for a divorce is natural, but it doesn't help you to move forward. It just forces you to dwell on the negative aspects of your confusing situation. You need to get on with living your life. Remember that parents divorce because of their problems, not because of what you or your siblings have said or how you all have behaved.

TAKE GOOD CARE OF YOURSELF

Your parents will be your parents for the rest of your life. Divorce won't ruin your family—it will change your family. When you are upset and feeling hurt or vulnerable, it is especially important to take good care of yourself. Here are some examples of nice things you can do for yourself:

- Go for a walk or a bike ride.
- Listen to your favorite music.
- Read a good book or your favorite magazine.
- Hang out with some friends.
- Watch a movie.

Playing video games with your friends can help you through some difficult emotional times during a divorce. Try to do fun and relaxing activities during periods of downheartedness.

BLAMING YOUR PARENTS FOR SPLITTING UP THE FAMILY

You might be very angry with both parents for splitting up your family, and you might blame them both equally. These feelings are very common, and it might take you a while to get over them. During the separation and divorce you need to be able to talk to your parents about how you are feeling. You can help the entire family when you talk about your fears and your emotions. Communicating with all the family members will help you have a sense of self-awareness and provide both you and the family members with an understanding of how the situation is affecting your feelings and behavior. In addition, talking to a counselor can help you all in channeling your emotions in a positive and productive way. Counseling might also enable you to feel like you are in control of yourselves during a time of much upheaval.

CHAPTER THREE

TALKING TO SOMEONE WHO UNDERSTANDS

F amilies that go through divorce frequently find that their whole world has changed. For teens, this change in their family can be one of the most heartbreaking and challenging losses they can encounter. When your parents divorce, your emotions can seem overpowering. You don't need to face your feelings alone. Talk to someone you trust. Ask your parents to set aside time to talk to you about the divorce. Tell them what you are feeling. Explain your concerns. Try to listen to what they have to say, too. The divorce isn't easy for them, either. Some young people find it difficult or even impossible to talk to their parents about divorce. In that case, they may want to find someone else to talk to, too.

COUNSELORS, PSYCHOLOGISTS, AND SOCIAL WORKERS

Counselors, psychologists, and social workers are professionals who are trained to talk to people about their problems. They can help you and your parents communicate with one another. You might want to talk to the counselor alone, too. Counseling can help you think about, express, and sort out your painful feelings.

Counselors, therapists, and social workers are trained to help families during emotional crises. They can help family members in understanding their feelings and communicating them to others.

Sometimes schools have a psychologist and social worker available to students to help them understand their feelings and can refer you to other professionals if you need to seek additional help. School guidance counselors can also provide some personal counseling and can put you in touch with support groups and professionals who might be able to help in keeping lines of communication open and discussions honest.

OTHERS WHO CAN LISTEN

Besides school counselors, psychologists, and social workers, you could also talk to a trusted adult, such as a favorite relative,

Some young people feel comfortable talking about family issues with their coaches. Others believe they can get objective opinions and inspiration from ministers or peer support groups.

teacher, neighbor, or nurse. It might be most helpful to seek out people who can be objective and neutral about your situation. Sometimes close family members are too subjective or emotionally wrapped up in your family's situation to be able to offer you objective, neutral advice. They might feel some loyalty to one parent more than the other. You should be able to find people who can be objective listeners and can provide encouragement and support. You might also consider talking to your coach, minister, or rabbi. In addition, some teens find it helpful to talk to their peers. Do you have a friend whose parents are divorced? It feels good to relate to people who understand what you are going through.

Luckily, there are helpful organizations all over the world set up just to help young people deal with divorce and other tough issues. Many of these agencies create peer support groups—groups where young people can talk to other kids and teens about divorce.

RAINBOWS FOR ALL CHILDREN

Rainbows for All Children is an organization that works with schools, churches, social agencies, and community groups to form peer support groups for children and teens dealing with the pain of divorce, death, and other family changes, including separation from a parent through military deployment. Rainbows gives kids the opportunity to share their experiences in structured settings where they can have complete freedom in expressing themselves and begin on the road to healing.

Roma Downey is a former star of the TV show *Touched by an Angel* and was once an honorary chairperson of Rainbows. "Change can be frightening," says Downey. "It is particularly difficult for children who don't understand what's happening. Grieving children need caring, trustworthy, and knowledgeable adults to whom they can turn. Rainbows teaches that pain of loss doesn't have to hurt forever."

Rainbows for All Children has specially trained people who support young people who are going through their grieving or separation processes.

BOOKS AND OTHER RESOURCES

You might find that reading can offer you a better understanding of the complicated issues surrounding separation and divorce. Reading articles and books might also be able to offer you some insight into how your parents feel and what they are grappling with as they go through the divorce process, too. There are many articles and books (fiction and non-fiction) available, both online and in your school and local libraries that can help you to deal with all the aspects of what you are feeling and experiencing during this challenging time. Remember that your school or local librarian is an important resource who can help you find information on the topics of separation and divorce. There are numerous self-help titles that can provide some support to you for grasping the issues and effects of your circumstances.

USING ONLINE SITES AND STAYING SAFE

On the Internet, there are many websites, chat groups, social networks, and support groups just for kids and teens to talk to one another about separation, divorce, and other issues. In addition, it is very easy today to stay in touch with friends and family members by communications such as Skype, FaceTime, e-mail, tweets, and instant messages.

Online support groups can provide forums for expressing your emotions and finding out about how others have handled similar situations during the divorce process.

Tim, fifteen, attends a middle school in Iowa. "My parents got divorced when I was seven," he says. "I never thought it bothered me that much. I felt like I could handle it, like, I was Superman or something!

"About three years ago, I discovered an Internet chat group for kids of divorce. I realized that I never talked about my feelings about the divorce because I was embarrassed. I felt like no one would understand. Online, nobody knew who I was and I could talk freely. I even discovered feelings that I didn't even know I had.

"I talked to kids about how we've used our parents, who feel guilty about having gotten a divorce, to get stuff that we want, like a new cell phone and clothes. I learned that manipulating my parents isn't cool. I recommend Internet groups to my friends whose parents are divorced. I tell them how it will make you feel better, even if you didn't know you felt bad in the first place!"

Tim's best friend, Christina, age fourteen, also found help online:

"For years after my parents divorced, I kept my feelings bottled up inside me. Then, after Tim told me about this chat group, I logged on, too. It amazed me how people who had never met me could be so helpful and supportive. Really nice kids from around the world gave me all sorts of good suggestions and information. I made a lot of online friends. I'm very thankful for the Internet."

When using the Internet, never give a stranger (or a new, online friend) any personal information such as your last name, address, phone number, Social Security number, or location of your school on your personal profile. Choose any online chat group or club very carefully. Select a site that has a good reputation. Make sure you have also set your profile to "Private" so that only the individuals that you know can have access to it. In addition, make certain that you are very careful about the type of information that you reveal to strangers online. Also make sure you are comfortable with sharing with the world the photographs, profile, and other information that you post on these kinds of sites.

HOTLINES

There are many telephone and website hotlines for young people who need to talk about divorce and other difficult issues. The people who work the hotlines have been trained to be confidential, caring, and helpful professionals. This person is someone who you can talk to about your problems and who can offer you feedback and guidance. Some young people prefer to call hotlines to talk about their feelings because they can remain anonymous—the hotline counselor doesn't need to know your real name to be able to help you. Many hotlines can give you access to a range of free services, including local resources that can offer help in crisis management, healing, and recovery, information about laws in your region, and emotional support in coping with feelings of loss, depression, or other issues.

CHAPTER FOUR

CAUGHT IN THE MIDDLE

During or after a divorce, you might find yourself in an awkward situation. You might find yourself being pulled between both parents. Divorce can make you feel as though you are being put to the test, that your loyalties are being divided, and that you are being asked to take sides. Being caught in the middle can result in new conflicting emotions. Kevin, fifteen, lives in Rhode Island. His mom and dad divorced three years ago.

> *"Whenever my parents would talk to each other, they would get in a big fight," says Kevin. "Then they quit talking to each other completely. After that I became the messenger—'tell your mother this' or 'tell your father I said blah blah.' What am I, their personal assistant or something? And I wish they wouldn't talk about each other when I'm around. They usually talk about each other to someone on the phone, and I overhear the conversation. Don't they realize I have ears? It makes me so angry!"*

TELLING YOUR PARENTS ABOUT HOW YOU FEEL

Divorced parents often make the mistake of talking about their former spouses within earshot of their children. They behave this way because they are angry and feel justified in putting down that person. However, it is not OK for one parent to talk negatively about your other parent in front of you. If one of your parents says something rude or negative about your other parent, don't try to block out what you heard or pretend it doesn't matter. Tell your mom or dad that you overheard him or her, and ask that person not to talk about your other parent when you are around. Tell that parent how his or her behavior

Sometimes, a parent doesn't understand how he or she makes you feel when that person speaks out against the other parent. You need to tell the parent that you are being put in an impossible position.

makes you feel. Some parents unconsciously seek their kids' help to support them in a conflict or to gain information about the activities of the other spouse. If your parent makes the mistake of asking you nosy questions about your other parent, it's time to speak up. After all, you cannot fix their marriage or help mend their relationship.

Tell your parent that you feel uncomfortable relaying information about your other parent. Ask that person to please talk to your other parent directly. Remember, parents are still learning, too. Express yourself. You will feel better, and hopefully, your parent will learn a lesson. It is not your responsibility to counsel one or both of them, and you'll just add to your own anxiety and stress by allowing yourself to be caught in the middle.

PLANNING WHAT YOU ARE GOING TO SAY

Sometimes it helps to have planned out what you want to say before you talk to your parent about your feelings. That way, you won't be at a loss for words. Jonathan gets very angry when his mom "puts down" his dad. But how can he tell his mom how he feels without making the situation worse?

JONATHAN: Mom, it hurts me, and makes me angry, when you talk about dad, because I love him, too. Please don't talk about him around me.

MOM: I didn't realize that it bothered you, Jonathan. I'm sorry, dear, I guess I wasn't thinking. I won't do that anymore.

Remember that keeping the lines of communication open and having honest exchanges with both parents will help calm fears and ease everyone's burden during the changing living situation.

CONFLICT RESOLUTION

Sometimes you can resolve conflicts between yourself and family members without much difficulty, but other times it can take a lot of effort to reach a resolution. Some conflicts will not be resolved. However, it's always beneficial to try to resolve conflict and to learn skills that can help you to solve problems and cope with the loss of your parents' marriage. The key is to listen to the different views in the situation. Don't interrupt the person when he or she is speaking about that person's point of view. You are trying to understand his or her thinking, and you will give that person the chance to understand yours, too. Next, you need to find some common ground. You need to discover some point or issue on which the two of you can agree. You also have to agree to accept some responsibility for the conflict or problem and seek areas in which you can compromise. Then you need to be committed to the relationship and the steps you need to take to maintain it. By taking these actions, you will be able to respond to resolve the conflict and avoid a future dispute.

ANGER AND ANGER MANAGEMENT

It is normal to feel anger and other intense feelings when your parents are divorcing, but there are both destructive and healthy ways to express anger. It is important to release your anger in ways that won't hurt you or anyone else. Some examples of destructive ways to show anger are hitting someone, breaking a window on purpose, or hurting yourself. Destructive anger can emotionally or physically hurt other people and it is not considered socially acceptable behavior. A healthy way to express anger is to scream into a pillow or hit the ground with a stick. Jogging or swimming can release angry tension. Although it is not always easy, you can learn to control anger and express it in constructive ways.

A healthy way to deal with the rage you might feel during a divorce is by participating in sports. Such activities can give you a constructive outlet for coping with some feelings of anger.

"One thing to do with anger is to use it to make a difference," says Lynn Namka, author of *How to Let Go of Your Mad Baggage*. "Take positive action with the momentum that anger gives. Life is about choices. You have choices about what to do when you get mad," says Namka.

Namka hosts a website called Angries Out, just for helping kids of divorce handle their anger. The website offers tips and strategies for decreasing anger and making better choices about what you can do whenever you feel yourself becoming angry.

CHAPTER FIVE

GETTING USED TO A NEW LIVING ARRANGEMENT

There are many issues that must be settled when a divorce happens. Your parents must resolve the issue of who will take care of the children and where and with whom the young people will live after the separation. There is physical custody and the day-to-day care of children. There is also legal custody, where one parent is given sole physical custody and usually the other parent has visitation rights. At times, parents agree to joint physical and legal custody of their children.

Sometimes young people have to go to court with their divorcing parents. If you have to go to court, you may have to speak to a judge. He or she will help your parents determine the best living arrangement for you and your siblings. Every family's post-divorce arrangement is different, but it is most common for a child to reside primarily with one parent and visit the other.

Family members might have to appear in court to determine what is in the child's best interest. It is customary for a child to live with one parent and spend time with the other.

KINDS OF CUSTODY

Matt is an Oregon middle school student. Since his parents' divorce a year ago, he and his sister, Denise, ten, spend half of their time with their father and half with their mother. This common legal arrangement is known as joint custody.

When a judge declares that a mom and dad will have full joint custody of their children, it means that the children will share their time equally with both parents. The parents will share care and responsibility for the children, including the children's education, health care, and other needs. The parents share both physical and legal custody of the children, and they have equal say in the children's welfare.

Occasionally, a judge will award custody to one parent. The other parent may or may not have visiting rights. Anne Wong, thirteen, was ten when her parents divorced. Her father remarried within months and moved to another state. A judge awarded Anne's mother sole custody of her daughter.

"I miss my dad, and I don't understand why he moved so far away," says Anne Wong. "It seems like he just cares about his new wife and stepson. I feel like I don't measure up. Everything has changed so much."

Usually in sole custody cases, the other parent has visitation rights, the legal right to visit and spend time with the child or children.

TESTIFYING IN COURT

It is very rare that a teen would be made to testify in court before a judge about which parent he or she would choose to live with.

What usually happens is that a professional is assigned to the case by the court and interviews the teen or child about his or her home life and emotions about the situation. The professional then writes a report and gives it to the court. The judge considers the professional's recommendations when making a decision.

Sometimes young people get to choose which parent will be their primary caretaker. This decision can put kids or teens in an awkward and even painful position. You may feel as if you are choosing sides and that you are being torn apart by your love and loyalty for both parents. You may even feel like you are betraying a parent. But you are simply making a decision based on what seems right for you at this point in time. It's natural to want to spend time with both of your parents or to have preferences that shift. For example, you may at first prefer to live with your mom. A couple of years later, you may choose to spend more time at your dad's place. It doesn't mean that you love one parent more than the other.

LIVING IN A SINGLE-PARENT HOUSEHOLD

Young people who live in single-parent households often get additional responsibilities. Their busy parent—not only a full-time parent but often employed outside the home—usually needs extra help around the house.

Bryan's parents divorced when he was nine. His dad accepted a job in another state. Bryan, now fifteen, has visited his dad only three times in the past six years. Bryan's mom basically raised him by herself.

"Because I grew up in a single-parent family I was given lots of additional duties," says Bryan. "Since I was ten years

Living in a single-parent household can mean that a teen will have to help with chores because the parent has to spend more time working at a job. It is good for young adults to learn how to contribute to a household so that they can help it succeed.

old, I've been doing my own laundry and bagging my own lunches for school. I even cook dinner most nights, when my mom has to work late. In a way, I don't think it was fair that I had to take on so many grown-up type responsibilities. But I can see that these chores and extra duties made me a more disciplined and trustworthy person. My mom trusted me to do a good job, to take responsibility, and I did."

Getting used to a single-parent household involves adjusting to many changes. You probably will be asked to take on new roles and tasks to help make the new home life a success.

TWO HOMES

Splitting your time between both of your parents can be hard. And long-distance, split custody arrangements can be especially tough on children. It might be awkward at first, but once you have established a routine, it can work out and you can still remain close to each member of your family. This arrangement allows both parents to be actively involved in your upbringing.

You'll have to create personal space at both homes. Try to surround yourself with things that make both places as much yours as you possibly can. You probably will have to duplicate some physical comforts at the two homes, but you will need to make the spaces feel like they are your home.

When dividing time between two homes, make sure you decorate both bedrooms to reflect your personality and help to put you at ease.

You will also need to learn the rules at each household. You'll need to know what is expected of you at each home, as well as what will be tolerated at each place. You will need to follow these rules even if you don't always agree with them.

REMARRIAGE AND STEPFAMILIES

Eventually, your divorced parent might remarry. If that happens, more big changes are coming your way. You will have a new stepmom or stepdad. Furthermore, if your stepparent has children, you will gain stepsisters or stepbrothers, too.

OH NO, MY PARENT IS DATING!

In time, parents may begin seeing new people and dating again. This change can be challenging for young people, especially when they still have secret hopes that their parents will reunite. It is natural to feel like you want to protect your parent and the relationship that you have with him or her. You might also find yourself comparing that new person with your other parent. The majority of people do remarry after divorce. According to the Pew Research Center, in 2013, almost forty-two million adults in the United States had been married more than once.

If your parents start to see other people or decide to remarry, you need to try to stay out of the middle of the new relationship. You might struggle with your feelings about being disloyal to your other parent if you like this new person too much. Give yourself time for the adjustment in accepting a new relationship within the family.

Stepfamily situations can be harmonious and happy. But, sometimes, getting along with a stepparent or stepsibling can be challenging. Personalities can clash, and conflicts can arise.

Stepfamilies, also called blended families, can also include stepsiblings, blood siblings (such as new children your parent and stepparent may have together), and sets of birth and step-parents. You probably will be going through many changes when you become part of a blended family. Eventually you will begin to gain your independence and forge your own identity.

Living in a blended family might be challenging in the beginning. Stepsiblings will need time to establish new family relationships and still maintain their individuality.

GETTING ALONG

With the formation of a new family unit, you might be wondering where you will fit in or how your daily life will be affected.

"I have really mixed feelings about my stepfamily," says Lidia, a middle school student from Ohio. "But there are good things about living in two houses, too. I have a cat at my mom's. At my dad's house I have a dog, a fish, and a parakeet. My dad remarried so I have a stepmom, too. But I also have a stepbrother, Rick, who's very mean and bossy. We get into fights and he grabs my things, and because he's much taller and stronger, I can't get them back. Then he just laughs at me. I can't stand him! My dad says I can't hit my stepbrother or even yell at him. He says I will have to adjust, but I don't want to. I only stay at my dad's place every other weekend, but, because of my mean stepbrother, I dread going to my dad's place sometimes."

Does your stepparent or stepbrother or stepsister do something that makes you really angry? Are you having a hard time dealing with differences between your stepsibling and yourself? If you don't work at resolving issues with your stepfamily, your problems will only continue. Conflicts should be resolved in a peaceful way. Fighting will only make things worse.

Talk to your stepparent or stepsibling, and tell him or her your feelings. Tell him or her how you want the situation to change. You may also want to talk to your mom and dad when stepfamily issues come up. When working out conflicts, it helps to work a compromise instead of a victory. Try to meet the other person halfway. If you try, you will probably find that there are peaceful solutions to the problems you are having.

CALLING FOR A FAMILY MEETING

Your teen years can be a tough time in your life to begin living with new people, especially if other teens are involved.

Lidia decided to talk to her dad about her issues with her stepbrother, Rick. She tried to stay calm as she explained the problem. She told her dad how Rick's behavior was making her not want to visit her dad's house. Her dad listened, and then he called the whole family together for what he called a powwow—a family meeting. At the meeting, Lidia told Rick exactly how his actions and behavior made her feel. Rick said he had just been trying to make her laugh, and he hadn't been trying to hurt her feelings or make her feel bad. He agreed to treat Lidia with more respect.

"I felt so relieved after we all talked," says Lidia. "I'm not 100 percent sure Rick will really stop being mean, but I'm willing to give him another chance. Things do seem better already."

Try to keep in mind that your stepsiblings are in a similar situation. They are trying to fit into the new, blended family, too.

GROWTH AND MATURITY

Change of any kind can be a challenge, and your parents' divorce can be one of the greatest challenges you will face in your life. Change brings you into unfamiliar territory. But you can also see change as an adventure—as an opportunity to learn and grow and take on new experiences. Because of your challenging experiences, you might even show a maturity in several ways, including the realization that stability, happiness, and security in a family are not guaranteed and that they should never be taken for granted.

Maybe you can't change your parents and make them married again, but you can change your attitude. You can choose to accept the divorce and not let it get in the way of your having a happy life.

As you go through your parents' divorce, try to be helpful to your parents and other family members. Be sure to ask for outside help when you need it. There are people who understand the feelings you are having, and they want to help you. Sometimes the ride will be a little bumpy, but you are going to be OK. If you can work at being open to new circumstances and responsibilities with the family, you will see new habits and routines emerge. Making the effort to work together to solve problems can help your new family situation be a positive one. Forgiveness, work, trust, honesty, communication, and love can put your newfound home life on a healthy course.

GLOSSARY

blended family A stepfamily whose members can include children of a prior marriage of one spouse or both.

compromise When two sides of a dispute come to an understanding by making a deal to meet each other halfway.

conflict resolution The process of finding solutions to a dispute that minimize the harmful consequences of the disagreement and are mutually satisfactory to both parties.

depression A mental condition characterized by prolonged feelings of sadness, hopelessness, worthlessness, or despair.

divorce The legal ending of a marriage.

joint custody Legal arrangement in which parents share decision-making about the care of the child.

physical custody An arrangement in which the child or children divide time between both parents after a divorce.

marriage The legal and/or religious union of two people.

maturity The state of having the emotional and mental characteristics of an adult.

separation When parents decide to live apart from each other. A "trial separation" lets them see what it is like to not be married anymore. Some parents get back together after a separation.

single-parent household A sole parent and a child or children living together as a family unit.

sole custody Arrangement in which one parent has complete responsibility for the child or children. Custody establishes with which parent a child or children will live after a divorce.

support group A group of people, sometimes led by a counselor or therapist, who agree to meet regularly to discuss a common issue such as divorce and support one another emotionally.

visitation rights Legal rules about how often the parent who does not have custody may see his or her children.

FOR MORE INFORMATION

Angries Out
10371 North Oracle
Pusch Ridge Center, Head Spring Office
Oro Valley, AZ 85737
(520) 825-4766
Website: http://www.angriesout.com
Started by Lynne Namka and managed by the company Talk,
    Trust & Feel, the Angries Out website offers information on
    ways to channel feelings of conflict and violence.

Children's Rights Council (CRC)
1296 Cronson Boulevard, Suite 3086
Crofton, MD 21114
(301) 459-1220
Website: http://www.crckids.org
The CRC works to help divorced, separated, and never married
    parents continue to be involved in their child's life.

Children's Defense Fund
25 E Street NW
Washington, DC 20001
(800) 233-1200
Website: http://www.childrensdefense.org
A national organization, the Children's Defense Fund advocates
    for children at the federal, state, and community levels by
    providing a voice for all children's needs.

Divorce Source, Inc.
P.O. Box 1580
Allentown, PA 18105-1580
(800) 680-9052
Website: http://www.divorcesource.com

An online network that provides information, websites, and support groups concerning divorce.

Families Change
Website: http://teens.familieschange.ca
Sponsored by the Justice Education Society of British Columbia, the website serves as a teen guide to what happens when parents separate and divorce.

Family Service Ontario
190 Attwell Drive, Suite 630
Toronto, ON M9W 6H8
Canada
(416) 231-6003
Website: http://www.familyserviceontario.org
This organization helps families and community organizations in Ontario and offers separation and divorce group programs.

Kids' Turn
(415) 777-9977
Website: http://www.KidsTurn.org
This group helps children in coping with parental separation and divorce. It provdes programs to help kids of all ages understand their emotions and find positive ways to express the feelings they have during separation and divorce.

The National Stepfamily Resource Center
Website: http://www.stepfamilies.info/about.php
This online center provides a list of US support groups and local chapters. On its website it offers links to organizations that can help in divorce support and legal issues.

Rainbows for All Children
1007 Church Street, Suite 408
Evanston, IL 60201
(847) 952-1770
Website: http://www.rainbows.org
This international nonprofit group assists young people who
   are grieving the loss of a loved one or who are experiencing divorce or some other life-changing crisis.

Hotlines
Teen Line
(310) 855-4673
This helpline is staffed by teens and adult volunteers who
   have been trained to provide outreach services.

Youth America Hotline
(877) 968-8454
This hotline helps young people who are in crisis.

WEBSITES

Because of the changing nature of Internet links, Rosen Publishing has developed an online list of websites related to the
subject of this book. This site is updated regularly. Please use
this link to access the list:

http://www.rosenlinks.com/FIY/Div

FOR FURTHER READING

Afineevsky, Evgeny. *What About Me?* (Teen and Divorce). DVD. Wheeling, IL: Film Ideas, Inc., 2014.

Bergin, Rory M., and Jared Meyer. *Frequently Asked Questions About Divorce* (FAQ: Teen Life). New York, NY: Rosen Publishing, 2012.

Espejo, Roman. *Custody and Divorce* (Teen Rights and Freedoms). Detroit, MI: Greenhaven Press, 2013.

Gay, Kathlyn. *Divorce: The Ultimate Teen Guide* (It Happened to Me). Lanham, MD: Rowman & Littlefield, 2014.

Hart, Joyce. *Frequently Asked Questions About Being Part of a Military Family* (FAQ: Teen Life). New York, NY: Rosen Publishing, 2010.

Iorizzo, Carrie. *Divorce and Blended Families* (Straight Talk About). St. Catharines, ON: Crabtree Publishing Company, 2013.

Marcovitz, Hal. *Teens and Family Issues*. Broomall, PA: Mason Crest Publishers, 2014.

Owens, Michael, and Amy Gelman. *I'm Depressed. Now What?* (Teen Life 411). New York, NY: Rosen Publishing, 2012.

Parks, Peggy J. *Teen Depression* (Diseases and Disorders). Detroit, MI: Lucent Books, 2013.

Peterman, Rosie L., Jared Meyer, and Charlie Quill. *Divorce and Stepfamilies* (Teen Mental Health). New York, NY: Rosen Publishing, 2013.

Quill, Charlie. *Anger and Anger Management* (Teen Mental Health). New York, NY: Rosen Publishing, 2009.

Schloat, Sara. *Getting Through It: Kids Talk About Divorce*. DVD. Mount Kisco, NY: Human Relations Media, 2014.

Simons, Rae. *Blended Families* (The Changing Face of Modern Families). Broomall, PA: Mason Crest, 2010.

Truly, Traci. *Teen Rights (and Responsibilities): A Legal Guide for Teens and the Adults in Their Lives*. Paradise, CA: Paw Prints Press, 2008.

INDEX

ABOUT THE AUTHOR

Jerry McLaughlin lives in Westchester County, New York. His parents were divorced when he was attending ninth grade.

Katherine E. Krohn is the author of several books for young readers, including *Everything You Need to Know About Birth Order* and *Everything You Need to Know About Living On Your Own*, and several celebrity biographies. She is a journalist and lives in Eugene, Oregon.

PHOTO CREDITS